MW00887895

Fall Plants

Julie Murray

Abdo Kids Junior
is an Imprint of Abdo Kids
abdobooks.com

Abdo
Kids

SEASONS: FALL FUN!

abdobooks.com

Published by Abdo Kids, a division of ABDO, P.O. Box 398166, Minneapolis, Minnesota 55439.
Copyright © 2021 by Abdo Consulting Group, Inc. International copyrights reserved in all countries.
No part of this book may be reproduced in any form without written permission from the publisher.
Abdo Kids Junior™ is a trademark and logo of Abdo Kids.

Printed in the United States of America, North Mankato, Minnesota.

052020

092020

THIS BOOK CONTAINS
RECYCLED MATERIALS

Photo Credits: iStock, Shutterstock

Production Contributors: Teddy Borth, Jennie Forsberg, Grace Hansen

Design Contributors: Candice Keimig, Pakou Moua, Dorothy Toth

Library of Congress Control Number: 2019955554

Publisher's Cataloging-in-Publication Data

Names: Murray, Julie, author.

Title: Fall plants / by Julie Murray

Description: Minneapolis, Minnesota : Abdo Kids, 2021 | Series: Seasons: fall fun! | Includes online
     resources and index.

Identifiers: ISBN 9781098202187 (lib. bdg.) | ISBN 9781098203160 (ebook) | ISBN 9781098203658
     (Read-to-Me ebook)

Subjects: LCSH: Autumn--Juvenile literature. | Fall foliage--Juvenile literature. | Seasons--Juvenile
     literature.

Classification: DDC 525.5--dc23

Table of Contents

Fall Plants

There are many different fall plants.

The carrots are ready.

Andy digs them up.

Meg plants pansies.

They will last all fall.

Mae picks apples.

She fills the basket.

Zane finds a maple leaf.

It is turning red.

Liam plants 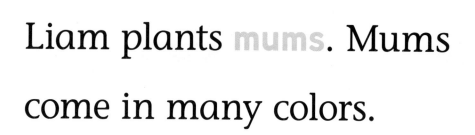mums. Mums come in many colors.

Elsa is on a hike. She sees a mushroom.

Eva sees the aspen trees.

The leaves are yellow.

Abe is at the pumpkin patch.

He picks out a big one!

More Fall Plants

birch

chokeberries

kale

sumac

Glossary

mum
short for chrysanthemum, a type of plant grown for its flowers that bloom in fall.

pansy
a garden flower that has flat, rounded petals that feel like velvet. Pansies grow in many colors.

Index

Abdo Kids ONLINE
FREE! ONLINE MULTIMEDIA RESOURCES

Visit **abdokids.com**
to access crafts, games,
videos, and more!

Use Abdo Kids code
SFK2187
or scan this QR code!